A clock-storm coming

Cinnamon Press

Books that are the spice of life

Published by Cinnamon Press
Meirion House
Glan yr afon
Tanygrisiau
Blaenau Ffestiniog
Gwynedd LL41 3SU
www.cinnamonpress.com

The right of the contributors to be identified as the authors of this work has been asserted by them in accordance with the Copyright, Designs and Patent Act, 1988. © 2006

ISBN 1-905614-24-1 (978-1-905614-24-0)
British Library Cataloguing in Publication Data. A CIP record for this book can be obtained from the British Library

All rights reserved. No part of this publication may be reproduced, stored in a retrieval system, or transmitted in any form or by any means, electronic, mechanical, photocopying, recording or otherwise without either the prior written permission of the publishers. This book may not be lent, hired out, resold or otherwise disposed of by way of trade in any form of binding or cover other than that in which it is published, without the prior consent of the publishers.

The exercise used by Carol Rumens during the course and referred to in the Foreword is from *Teach Yourself Writing Poetry and Getting Published* (London, Hodder & Stoughton, 1997) p.32.

Designed and typeset in Palatino by Cinnamon Press
Cover picture from original artwork © Martin Figura 2006
Cover design by Mike Fortune-Wood

Contents

Foreword by Carol Rumens	5
Scrimshaw by Sue Leigh	11
Miracle by Sue Leigh	12
Windblown by Sue Leigh	13
Boxes by Leontia Flynn	14
The Space Inside by Gill Nicholson	15
The Difficulty of Dying Beautifully by Gill Nicholson	17
Dawn by Gill Nicholson	19
Wasted by Gill Nicholson	20
A Lamp-post by Lindsay Fursland	21
Tea with the Emperor by Viv Appple	25
Learning Curve by Viv Apple	26
Pyjamas Of Hope by Viv Apple	28
Cypher by Helen Ivory	30
Storm by Helen Ivory	31
Rain by Helen Ivory	32
Storms and Clocks by Joan Michelson	33
Path to Paradise by Joan Michelson	34
Torch of Joy by Joan Michelson	35
The Horror Bucket by Martin Figura	36
Numbers by Martin Figura	38
Hot Day by Martin Figura	39
Polar Route by Jenny King	40
Wellie by Jenny King	41
Walking down a field by Jenny King	42
Map Making Jan Fortune-Wood	43
Finding a Rhythm by Jan Fortune-Wood	44
Bracketing by Jan Fortune-Wood	45
From 'The Unfinished' by Christopher Reid	46
London Stone by Carol Rumens	48
His grandmother Carrie by Mavis Howard	50

Tick by Mavis Howard	52
Joan Miro, Blue II, 1961 by Carole Coates	53
A clock-storm coming by Carole Coates	54
Mint by Judy Brown	56
Gifts by Judy Brown	57
Her Third Hand by Jennifer Copley	58
Weather by Jennifer Copley	59
Wardrobes by Jennifer Copley	60
A portrait of V Nubiola by Anne Berkeley	62
Telling the weather by Anne Berkeley	64
Letter composed on a typewriter by Rosie Blagg	65
Poem for a friend who skittered by Rosie Blagg	66
A Shyness of Torches by Rosie Blagg	67
Companions by Christy Ducker	68
Anchorage by Christy Ducker	70
Do Not Disturb by Christy Ducker	72

Foreword

Writing effective poems has to do with de-familiarisation. To present some relatively familiar thing in a way that grips and fires your reader, you have to have seen or felt it yourself with an especially intense surprise and, perhaps, a certain bafflement. Keats, in one of his many profound insights into the psychological states of the poet, said it was necessary to be 'capable of being in uncertainties, mysteries, doubts, without any irritable reaching after fact or reason…' Bringing a new group of poetry-minded people together in a new place on an Arvon course can hardly be part of what Keats had in mind: nevertheless, an 'Arvon' can be a little induction into various lesser but useful forms of 'negative capability.' A new group is electric with connections and cross-currents. Faces to remember, different sounds, a strange bed, possibly dreams to match. Breakfast with a struggle of your instant poetry-family. Reading solo for the first time in front of everyone. Getting slightly lost. Not hearing the News. Those familiar poems you carried with you begin to look different. New poems begin to look possible.

For four and a half days you're with companions and mentors - but also on your own. You're in a beautiful setting, in green sloping spaces superficially 'poetic' - but that guarantees nothing. You're committed to finding the unexpected – and to entering inner space. The course that this anthology celebrates took place during what must have been the hottest week of the summer of 2006. Butterflies hatched on the window-sills. We ate food like chocolate pudding and shepherds' pie for supper, and despite the distractions of the green shades and the ticking clock and the hot rooms, our group was focussed and alert and extremely hard-working. The tutors, Christopher Reid and I, and the sixteen students, were in the deliciously shadowy Foyle Studio at 9.30 sharp every morning, writing, close-reading, discussing poetry. There was a high level of professionalism among these advanced poetry students, many of whom had books in print, or about to be. No-one seemed jaded or superior. Every mind was available for surprise.

The poems here are a mixture of material written during the course, brought along as work-in-progress or produced in response to exercises. There are some lively pieces in the latter category. Exercises are useful irritants. With luck, they set free ideas you didn't know you had. They ask a playfulness which we don't always allow our goal-driven selves. It's often when you're not taking the poem too seriously, and certainly not being too self-critical in advance, that the subconscious mind throws you a snip of unexpected treasure.

Christopher gave the group 'clocks' and 'storms'- good, nourishing words, like the shepherds' pie and chocolate pud of the imagination. There was a terrific response, as readers will see. I offered a version of an exercise devised by Matthew Sweeney and John Hartley Williams in which people are randomly ascribed one abstract and one concrete noun. This liberated some quirky angles on everyday objects – and some comic talents. (We ought to remember how often we lost ourselves in laughter. And the occasional glass of wine. Oh yes, it wasn't only sestinas.)

To Jan Fortune-Wood for putting together this memento of a rather special course, to our guest Leonia Flynn and to all the students for their creative energy and enthusiasm, warmest thanks from Christopher and myself. There are new shapes on these page, new eyes behind new images. The clock ticks on in the clock-tower but the fresh words here will keep that summer green for a good while longer.

Carol Rumens, Wales, 07.09.06.

for Kerry, Peter and Pearl,
with thanks

A clock-storm coming

Scrimshaw
by Sue Leigh

We sighted them two winters out of Nantucket
at daybreak

their backs
miraculous grey islands

we hunted the plumes of their breath

for three days the harpoon waved like a flag
from her head

the sea bled

and when we had finished the flensing
the scraping, the scooping

we boiled the oil

(which smelled so sweet and burned so bright
and was the colour of straw)

then I saved for myself
a milk-smooth tooth

scratched with my sail needle
a likeness of this sloop

and with lampblack
I darkened my name.

Miracle
by Sue Leigh

Today I saw two swallows on a wire –
and I remembered
how they fly from the veldt
of southern Africa
over the hot bowl of the Sahara
above the snow line of the Pyrenees
through Gascony, Poitou
Anjou, Normandy
across the grey waters
of the English Channel
and the soft blowing weald of Kent
just to lay their four white eggs
in our shed again

Windblown
by Sue Leigh

I imagine all the winds of the world
out of the bag

the Blue Norther
Buran, Bull's Eye Squall

Piterak, Chinook

the Steppenwind

and the Simoon heavy with dust

leaving behind its glitter of sand
on the tent-dwellers -

as this small gust
comes in at my window

leafing through my life

Boxes
by Leontia Flynn

A grey-clad official at a customs desk
-- by the outbound flights, or in some border town --
bends on your passport like a feeding bird
on the worm of your struggling ... indigestible name.

A sudden light come on in his eagle eye.
He hauls out reams of white, official forms,
a set of bathroom scales, a measuring tape,
a fingerprint kit, a pot of black ballpoint pens.

There are boxes to tick for your name, age, destination
fields to be filled for your income! the length of your instep!
-- and the usual cries of 'nothing to declare,'
on the part of the detained – tired and indignant.
You write "Yes Please" for sex?; and "Northern Irish" – "N. I."
Which also, privately, stands for "N(ot) – I(nterested)...".

The Space Inside
by Gill Nicholson

I had picked a columbine,
with all the loveliness, she said,
of pink and yellow butterflies.

I pierced and blew a fresh goose egg
its yolk and white a mottled glue
mixed in a bowl, for omelettes.

While she was out I sketched the flower
selected colours and my brush
transferred the image to the curve.

The egg was clean yet not quite smooth.
I held it brittle in my hand
thought of her skin, her heavy breast.

Those hours of painting were, perhaps
the happiest I've ever spent.
I made a tiny scroll to say

how much I loved her, rolled it tight
and pushed it through the minute hole
concealed, yet, by its rattle, known.

We set it on the rosewood shelf
kissed and later made long love
as I intended, hoped we would.

What sparked the storm?
What had been said
to bring such bile into my throat?

Wasn't I her only one,
ever, always in her past?
Before she knew me, even then,
wasn't I her only one?

Unreasoned and unreasonable
that she should have a space for me
where I alone, and only I, could be.

Caught in the headlights of my rage
she smashed the egg against the wall
made hard-edged fragments of the flower.

The scroll I thought she'd never see
she took and read, tossed it aside.
I saw her writhe, her disbelief, her grief.
My anger drained, I felt her pain and cried.

The Difficulty of Dying Beautifully
by Gill Nicholson

My chrysanthemums have thick stems
and tough leaves. Their white petals
radiate from a secret centre
like luminous fireworks.
They have lasted six weeks,
yet over the last three
their spiky grip has loosened
their heads gone awry;
they are not pristine
though they suck up water
by the inch.

*

May is frail, wobbly on her feet
slow in speech, her skin pale
crumpled like white tissue paper
for throwing away.
Bewildered to see us,
we take her in the garden.
She is full of fresh wonderment
when she sees the trees:
cedar of Lebanon, acacia
and copper beech that cast huge shadows.
I wonder who planted those? she says.

They're over a hundred years old
Guy says. *Victorian gardeners planted
such precious saplings carefully.*
May listens. Then she says
I wonder who planted those trees?
She does not want us to leave.

*

Shake the chrysanthemums
gently
bury the petals
now.

Dawn
by Gill Nicholson

It speckles open throated birds
dazzles bubbles as the salmon leaps,
fox reflects his pink tongue,
caved bats wait patient, up-side-down.

It haunts the corners of her eyes
scratches tallies in white chalk
nags an ant-hill of questions,
thoughts adamant as diamonds.

It heaves sulphurous breath
forces a no turning back
holds her by the scruff of the neck,
her tangled scalp its trophy.

Bone on bone, she is log-jammed
in the spate of morning.

Wasted
by Gill Nicholson

Flesh fell away,
his six-foot frame
held by skin and sinew
so frail, his complaint became
the hard shell
of his breakfast egg.
My mother lifts the sheet
gently, so as not to disturb
his last shocking breaths,
shows me his bones.

A Lamp-post
by Lindsay Fursland

It's a quarter past three at the opening
To a hazeless morning in May,
Stars are still just about happening
As hedgehog and skylark hold sway,

When out of the remnant of night-time
A missionary figure appears
Who's pulled to this place like a magnet
Like she's been for seventeen years.

Fortnightly she buys from the garage
To re-prove she bore a son
Two bunches of votive chrysanthemums,
Two for the price of one.

She binds them bright to the lamp-post,
Fresh in the sleepless dusk,
Marking the spot where her baby
Became a mortal husk.

Gary's dad's a D-Day statistic,
A name bereft of a grave;
Stopping a random bullet
He fell asleep in a wave.

Gary's the spit of his father:
Danger runs in the genes;
Rejection is what he's good at,
Though it's not what Gary means.

His mother drowns him with loving;
Gary's her sole souvenir.
He can only breathe in desertions
Because she comes too near.

She buys him a bike for his birthday,
Praying to lighten his mood:
He centaurs into the saddle,
A hurtling ingratitude.

He's clad in obligatory leathers,
Affecting a dark-angel black:
Trousers/boots/gauntlets; his jacket
Says NOMAD in stars on the back.

His helmetlessness is a V-sign
To an unheroic age;
Scathed by a dragonless lifestyle
Which only speed will assuage.

On the A1 before they improve it
He dares the lights on red,
Disdaining to brake at all crossroads,
He leaves patrol-cars for dead.

An underage damsel rides pillion,
Enthralled, roaring into the sun;
Peroxide streaming behind her,
Young Sharon from next-door-but-one.

Sharon loves Gary's defiance
And his sulking she's learned to dispel
By asking nothing – just chewing
And feigning indifference as well.

Only Gary played chicken with lorries
As the life inside him glowed,
Risking juggernaut-doom by a whisker
When crossing the Great Cambridge Road.

His bike possesses him utterly
As its engine begins to hum;
Its revs sing sweeter to him
Than Sharon or even his mum.

She purrs like a panther at sixty,
At eighty she growls like a lion;
At a ton a cacophonous banshee
Turns your soul to iron.

Nothing feels true as that union
Of body and mind and machine;
You feel a king of the highway,
Your bike is your trustiest queen.

Past Barnet he blurs like a bullet
Through dormant Botany Bay,
Meteoric down ghostly B-roads
Fast-forwarding fortune away.

Careering round to the Black Spot,
Which was why they'd put the light there,
(Its lantern's been dead for a fortnight
And is still awaiting repair),

On a trivial slip-road to Enfield
Where the oak tree blinded the bend
Gary lost track of its swerving
And quickly beholds it's the end.

The lamp-post is skewed by the impact,
It leans at thirty degrees,
Resuscitating the lantern
Which suddenly brightens the trees:

He seems like a shadow akimbo,
Tucked up in the leaves and the mud;
And with hair as red as he dyes it
You nearly don't notice the blood.

For as long as flowers will open
And as long as hearts may be torn,
She will draw to that fatal vertical
With garlands to freshly adorn.

Ever-revving around that corner
His restless Triumph vrooms.
Ever-wreathing that lethal lamp-post
Her loss continually blooms.

Tea with the Emperor
by Viv Appple

'As you can see,
I've been shopping
at the Royal Academy.
Excuse the mess.

'Oh, mind your head on that foot.
Yes, Damien at his best, I think,
exposing hypocrisy –
a snip at thirty grand.

'This piece is a nice contrast of texture.
Says a lot about density, don't you agree?
Had to remove the library doors to get it in
but I feel that it was worth the effort. Sold
a few books to raise the ninety thousand.
We call it the headless hedgehog –
all five tons of it.

'Do have a biscuit. NO! – not those!
Can't you see how they're arranged?
It's called "Human Sexuality" you understand.
And very sensitively done.

'That picture I'm particularly proud of.
Lovely, isn't she? Everyone says so.
Direct and simple, sitting there in her LBD.
What? The arm join with the sleeve isn't quite right?
No, I don't think you can be looking properly.
It won the RAA Award for most distinguished exhibit.
As with all these things, you have be in the know.

'More tea?'

Learning Curve
by Viv Apple

Standing on the back step,
(Was I four or maybe five?)
I held the teddy tight,
destruction on my mind.

That small tear in his tummy
was his downfall:
my invitation to experiment.
I pulled a tiny bit of light, white stuffing
from the ragged hole
and held it up to catch the wind,
let go, and watched it soar

over a bush by the back gate,
passing the dustbin – just –
then, with a sudden lift,
it cleared the fence
and floated on, away.

I stared in fascination, hooked,
and pulled another piece
from that sad bear, launching
the childish handful with an eager arm,
watching it follow the firstborn –
now a spec above the garage roof.

I was a junkie now,
filling the air and sky
with the detritus of my drunk delight

until at last, all stuffing spent,
the bear lay still and quiet
in my arms.

But drugs are strong
and won't let go so easily. Thereafter,
every seed head from a dandelion clock
which floated by
I'd try to recognise
and say to anyone who'd listen, baffled,
'Look – there goes my piece of fluff!'

awareness of my self-delusion
creeping up on me

Pyjamas Of Hope
by Viv Apple

Yes, I thought of you, my love,
when I bought those pink pyjamas,
those pretty pink pyjamas
with the white lace trim

for you'd gone off in a huff, love,
while I chose those pink pyjamas;
shopping's not your favourite sport
and you were looking very grim.

So I took a pair of scissors
to those lovely pink pyjamas,
cut the legs off pretty sharpish
– and the lacy bit of trim.

Now the top appeared top-heavy
so I shortened both the sleeves
on my delightful pink pyjamas
that I'd bought upon a whim

and to make them even nicer,
those perfect pink pyjamas,
I cut out a plunging neckline,
stitched it with the white lace trim.

Then I threw away the buttons
on my newish pink pyjamas
so you wouldn't have to struggle
when the lights were dim.

But now they look like a disaster,
my sorry pink pyjamas,
so you'll find me in the pink -
without a trace of lacy trim.

Cypher
by Helen Ivory

Her weight suspended in air
casts no shadow on the wooden floor.
Light spills from the open window,
spells out the shape of her face,
the line of her arms, belly,
the ridge of a scar, her hands.

This is pure language,
played from frame to frame
until a complete sentence is constructed,
making sense of all this unused space.
Still this chill passes over her,
presses its fingers to her neck, counts her pulse

Storm
by Helen Ivory

A fat, manageable word.
Pick it up like a brick,
put it down anywhere.
Then see what happens.

The clocks unwind,
shower seconds
and minutes like seeds
into air.

Some take root in crop fields,
carve lives for themselves
as corn spirits,
roughing-up neat lines.

Some become sea-sprites,
take pleasure in building up
waves, until big enough
to drown the land.

Many take to the desert,
measure hours and grains
of sand, fling it all upon
tented towns and farms.

When storm has done its work
there is an inescapable quiet.
A halting of breath, of heartbeats,
an ocean of night upon night.

Rain
by Helen Ivory

It rains. The world is at a tilt.
The house where the clock-maker lives
clings to the edge of a slate hill.
The clock-maker left on Tuesday.

Inside the house of the clock-maker
is carnage. The innards of a thousand
corpses lie on a giant table, some spilled
on the floor. By and by, a hand twitches.

It rains, a litany of rain upon slate roofs.
Nobody has noticed the clock-makers house
is still, so lost in their own stillness are they.
Nobody has noticed the absence of moon.

The clock harnessed to the front
of the clock-makers house keeps an eye
on the grey valley. It is tired
and now only counts every second minute.

As it darkens, the heft of hills inch closer,
wearing night like a cloak of themselves.
And still, rain fills the valley,
rises to cover the clock's watching eye.

Storms and Clocks
by Joan Michelson

The storm of dawn at five am
restores the hill of spruce
and from the earth
the stubble of a field that springs
as if there's set right here
a clock
and with the waking of the sheep,
it shakes, it burrs and silent,
it goes off.

Path to Paradise
by Joan Michelson

Kerry carries the Torch of Joy
for us to cook for Thursday dinner
in this manner. Rub with Herbs
of Bliss, say garlic, sage and mint.
Bake together with the sister
Torch of Terror left to stew
in its own juices for United
Vegans and the Purist Veggies.
For them, unsalted and undressed,
also Leaves of Love and Fruit
selected from the Bowl of Mercy.
Then toast Crusts of Sloth for Regs,
dissolve the Nails of Discord in hills
of Shropshire Blue, a cheese with Veins
of Lunacy that treats the belly
to a Sleep of Grief. And bake.
And wait. And wait for after supper
poems with the Flowerpots
of Justice and the wooden benches
and the Pearl of Girl who charms,
experimenting with our words,
now hers mixed up in children's songs.
Readings begin after-supper.
By then, both torches have been eaten,
the dishes racked and the Jacket
of Distress hung on the Hook
of Hurst House Manor alias Heaven.

Torch of Joy
by Joan Michelson

Too hot to hold, the Torch of Joy
is tossed from hand to hand
around the room
and out into the world
where fire blooms
and innocents with lust
take hold as if they have no soul
and never felt
the branding
mark of Trespass.
Somewhere lies a law
that fire in water
also leaves a scar.

The Horror Bucket
by Martin Figura

The dark trip down the backyard
past the Anderson Shelter
to where the bogey man stood guard
was too much in the winter.

So the Horror Bucket, as it was known,
spent the night on the landing
lowering the tone.
From autumn to spring.

through the hours of sleeping
children tinkled and adults pissed.
The level forever deepening
and if we were lucky, nobody missed.

Each morning one of us children
took their turn , a job we did gingerly
contents kept in the bucket, then
chucked down the privy

Friday was father's night out
He'd clatter in late
kick the bucket and shout.
Then let go, a river in spate.

One time he let his trousers fall
took off his hat
slid down the wall
then very heavily sat.

and treated us to a trumpet solo
that when it finally came to a stop
(and this is more than you want to know)
was followed, not by applause, but a plop.

Numbers
by Martin Figura

So this is what I'm good at.
My class mates drown
in the five times table, while I
race on in my head:

> five seventeens are eighty five;
> six seventeens are one hundred and two.

I am a number, a sharp yellow seven
I think: Prime and primary.
This is something that sets me apart.
I'm not sure what it means yet.
I don't know that numbers
are not ruled by laws, that they are the law.
Music, poetry, painting, cricket,
money, sex, the Big Bang – it all
comes down to numbers.

Hot Day
by Martin Figura

I stoop through the brambles
into a scratched photograph
Along the path, shirtless boys
are wet from the river.

The pool I swam in
forty years ago is dry;
the ground parched, broken apart.
I reach down, put my fist into it.

Polar Route
by Jenny King

The bus halts, shakes my thoughts
into a different pattern.
Trees at the tennis club start to shed their leaves:
the season's changed.

Halfway, or near enough,
looking down miles from the plane that long-past year,
we saw ice-peaks, frozen ridges, and I sang
that hymn-line about Greenland, quietly,
surprised – it was the first day of September.
Arrived, we walked through cactus gardens, arboretum,
test-shook the grapefruit tree.
Drove out in quest of desert, little towns
moon-distant from our knowledge. Never looked

into the slow revolve of our own lives,
so eager to stare outwards.
                                      The bus moves on,
takes the slow hill where we came once to view,
house-hunting, years before the trip.
Halfway up here, below our house, they told us
there's a snow-line we'd see when winter came.
We didn't credit it, but now we do.

Wellie
by Jenny King

Out from the overgrown ditch beside the path
a small child climbs to greet me.
"Look!" she says. We have never met.
She wants to talk, holds up a goose-grass ribbon.
"It's sticky!" I stop. She scrambles off once more,
comes back with a snail and a smile.

Her picnicking family, a few yards off,
glance, register, ignore.

The last offering's best. She's bringing water
scooped in her wellie, plods in one boot, one sock;
before she's reached me, stops, peers in amazed.
"There's things." I ask to look but she's intent,
then turns away. "There's things!" she calls again,
hobbling to her dad. I am discharged; walk on.

Walking down a field
by Jenny King

On the diagonal,
swallows flitting and chittering
at odd angles out of the sky's corners

and my thoughts
gathering from every direction
without pattern

or none that I can see
though the birds as they loop and twist
never collide I think

about time about
people and change and everything
under the sun.

I turn sideways to pass through the wall-gap
into tree shade.
There at the wood's heart I will consider

the weight of existence,
but at the last minute I understand
the swallows' method,

how comings and goings are what define position,
how the centre of a life
is best understood in corners.

Map Making
by Jan Fortune-Wood

An edge of flag –

unfurling at the limits
of these downcast names,

borders blending muffled
green to sliding
grey to muted
beige.

And to the west, the margin
of a ragged land
frays
into a tattered sea
that will not let me
sink.

A sullen scrawl of hieroglyphs.
A discord of unspoken dreams –

Nothing
to declare.

Finding a Rhythm
by Jan Fortune-Wood

In the minutes before the storm
our skin prickles. Sweat. Heat pooling
in the cup of your palm against my spine.

We watch the clock,
listen for thunder
cleaner than incense.

A cloud folds into itself, timpanies
against the air, shudders like
muscle over-reaching its stretch. The light
slices
the dark.

Now comes the rain:
it pounds the night –
systolic pulse,
diastolic throb,
bodhrán skin under spilling
grain, the squall's
heart-beat
making
our pace.

Bracketing
by Jan Fortune-Wood

At Laycock we emerge from Talbot's shrine
to yellow sun on yellow stone,

the bees and your unbounded spiel
buzzing in the pregnant heat.

You aim and snap, capture something
fathomless while I fall in and out of

focus, hear the words – *perspective, format,
depth of field*, but miss the sentences.

As you zoom out I reel my shutters in,
narrow down the aperture and, without film,

catch the flutter of our secret son.
Later, gowned and numb under the lights,

the fast retort of your motor-wind comforts
me. You bracket every take, but cannot

frame the infinite shock of this ancient
conjuring trick: his body lifted from mine

like flesh broken from flesh.

From 'The Unfinished'
by Christopher Reid

A warm croissant
and cappuccino
were our morning rite:
alternate bites
of flaking, buttery pith;
then the straw guided
into her mouth
and the coffee making
its hesitant ascent
with puckered sucks
that just as stutteringly subsided.

Tougher work
than playing an oboe,
yet performed with a gusto
that customarily took
more than her fair share.
Not that I was measuring!
Rather, it was a case
of pride and delight
in such simple pleasuring:
the look on her face,
pure, animal appetite.

Therefore, not heart-breaking,
to picture her
across a table
in some quiet French seaside spot,
scanning a cluttered
plateau de fruits de mer
with its full surgical couvert,
and about to clatter
her way through the lot
as slowly as she was able.

London Stone
by Carol Rumens

They were young, war was new, it was nylons
and lippie, and drinks on the house
in the Strand, in a place called the Coal Hole.

They drank Gin and It till they spun,
and the warrior, scrubbing her kiss
with his wet, red knuckle, ran

over the cobbles to Charing Cross Station
where soldiers were roaring like coal
down the dirty old throat of the coal-hole,

and the warrior's woman decanted
her drink in the palm-pot and swayed
through the dawn with the glow of a bride

already, to win the new war,
a stone's throw away, where the poor were,
where it licked up the high streets, still hungry.

London, you can't have forgotten.
Haven't your books got no pages –
or did you just rip out the pages

about what the bombs do in bomb-holes,
the cute little fox in his fox-hole,
and the hero who hoots from the hell-hole.

The bartender's sixty years late, wasn't born.
though he knows the word, Blitz - it's a cocktail,
and everyone's sixty years late and not born

and we go with the flow in the Coal Hole,
where nothing's been changed since the Tudors
and history's only a tart with no heart

in her brass and mahogany boudoir,
making the poor blighters poorer.
So where's the way out? And the hole,

the hole we go down in, and when's
the train coming, the train we go home in
after we've started the stoning?

Stone is the way, let me show you.
Stone, where no stone was before.
Stone from the optics and fountains,

stone for the walkers and sleepers,
stone for the strikers, the same for the suckers,
stone for their bodies to melt in,

stone for the myth to be built on.

Stone for the soot-flakes to fall on

when all the stone has fallen.

His grandmother Carrie
by Mavis Howard

My father told the stories as if they were true.
How they danced at the top of Carrie's house,
fell through the ceiling. My grandmother,
Carrie's daughter, tutted. In a voice
of indignation she rebuked our laughter.
'Not true.' We knew. Believed at the same time.

Carrie was remote from any time
that we had known. This made her more true.
My father the jester wielded laughter
like a multicoloured flag in our house.
My mother demurred in a passive voice,
but he was as roguish as his grandmother.

We longed to have known this grandmother,
gone now in the downward spiral of time.
She paddled in her bloomers, and her voice
at the pictures was the loudest. It is true
that she bought on the black market, so her house
was full of sugar and ham. Our laughter

pushed my father to new heights. His laughter
as he drove the tales of his grandmother
to fresh extravaganzas brightened our house.
While mother was anxious about meals on time,
being good and patient, really true
to principles, speaking nicely, his voice

grew more daring, slightly coarser, Carrie's voice
and his a duo of unseemly laughter.
I desperately needed Carrie to be true.
We envied him this wonderful grandmother
who bet on greyhounds, broke our rules. Bedtime
Carrie stories were paradise in our house.

We grew up and Carrie swaggered from the house.
Write them down, I said. Mmm, he said. His voice
is silent as Carrie's now. That passage of time
has passed. But my father's reckless laughter
and the tales of his swashbuckling grandmother
still shout in my childhood memories as true.

My child has bedtime stories. Not Carrie. Laughter
is softer in this house. I can't do my father's voice
or that of his grandmother. I can't get them true.

Tick
by Mavis Howard

My childhood alarm rang an hour behind.
The churchyard sundial works part-time.

The grandfather, the pendulum? All that
whitebeard sickle stuff? Forget it.

Count the seconds between flash and crash?
A few drops. Not here. Not now.

Greenwich goes on being consistent,
the speaking clock platitudinous.

Tears are natural, relieve the tension.
Waves are for surfing, tsunamis the exception.

White unto harvest? At the first stroke?
Red dye covers the damage.

Voices play prophet in Trafalgar Square
(warglobalwarmingreligion). I carry an umbrella.

Take the Rolex to the watchmaker. It's running
too fast, too loud. You have the guarantee.
Let him see to it.

Lightning. Go indoors. Hide under the stairs.
Put in your earplugs. Count very slowly.

Joan Miro, Blue II, 1961
by Carole Coates

blue blue blue is all adjective ambitious adjective but it hasn't made it yet - become a noun I mean and I'm trying to help it but it doesn't help me there's no up no down no prepositions - those twelve adjectives of black or are they nouns like blobs or rocks could be sitting in a row or falling – if it was clear I could claim a verb – I'm trying to make this thing into a sky or a sea although the long red adjective which is on the left or the bottom is a thuggish red - a ruffian on the stairs red – and won't easily become a sail or a kite - but I'll place an imaginary ladder and open a window in the blue and tell myself I hear wind, waves, larks - smell strong Atlantic gusts - it is blue after all but perhaps a stronger blue than Cornwall – no it's cicadas I hear, smell thyme on the Peloponnese – I can dress myself in wings and a tail and say this is Ephesus - but the blue remains irreducibly cobalt - a colour from a tube - the black is ivory black or ink spots although the red is still a scream in the night – no it's a streak of vermilion – and I am a woman stuck on an imaginary ladder in fancy dress trying to help three colours become a narrative – or even just a sentence – but the title suggests progress - two could become three or five – a noun and a verb perhaps – but then look at the date – if you read it back to front it's still the same

A clock-storm coming
by Carole Coates

I live in a clock prison,
sleep in a limestone crack
of the clock wall, the giant
timepiece behind my head.
It grunts to me, minute by minute,
belches hourly, teaches me
everything I know.
CHRONOMETRY CLEPSYDRA CHRONOGRAPH
If I nod, it becomes
inconsequential, lapses
into a fugue, rattles alarmingly.
HOURGLASS SANDGLASS PENDULUM
It's a handsome clock, I believe,
but my horizon is a huge beam
which shifts when I look at it, slides away,
makes my dim cell spin until I'm sick.

I live in a clock prison
but watch the slit of unimportant sky.
The weather tells me what to do.
It postulates vehemence,
recommends a storm.
I shall concern myself with rain and lightning.
Thunder is harmless and can be left
to somebody less angry.
ADJUST MARK TIME SYNCHRONISE
Wind is also necessary
and shall be attempted.
It must be strong as limestone.

I am making solid rain
and that lightning which leaps up from the ground.
GONG BELL SIREN
I am locked in a clock making storms.

Mint
by Judy Brown

At school, she heard, there were girls
with a ring-shaped decay on the slope

of a molar. Their sweets burrowed
into enamel as sea urchins do

into rock. Her parents warned her:
Danger can take many forms.

At forty-five, the sound
of those pennies is starting

to thunder, a coiny Niagara.
She's starting to see the marks

of teeth on her nails, of time
on her teeth. How the world leaked in

(or out) through the hole in the mint.
If she'd dared to put her eye

to its arctic pupil, she might
have viewed in high resolution

the price she'd pay for leaving
her brace on the bedside table,

its whorled pink glass pierced
with wires like something electric.

Gifts
by Judy Brown

You told me this: At the gunfire
escape of jellybeans out of the jar
that needed two hands to lift, into the scoop
of the scales, chrome coming away
from the dun underneath, the jellybean seller,
the sweet shop man, shivered and said:
>   *I hate that sound.*

I remembered this: When the boys
were young, we teaspooned rice
into balloons. The sound was rain
on an old metal roof, a scribbled spring river
rioting in soakaways, a mad drumming.
You turned to me, shivered and said:
>   *I love that sound.*

Her Third Hand
by Jennifer Copley

is the one which pinches, steals.
It uncurls from between her shoulder-blades
when the coast is clear.
She wishes she had an eye in the nape of her neck
then she would know when it was waking up
but nine times out of ten she is ready for it,
never turning her back on the things it likes.

Occasionally it outwits her
and she lands home with a ring in her pocket,
a bracelet down her jumper;
the flashier the better, it has no taste.

One of these days she'll be caught
by a store detective, she thinks
so she stops going into town,
orders shopping over the net,
bids for things on e-bay.
The hand sulks, itches her
in places she can't reach.

Sometimes she caves in,
sits with her back against the dressing-table,
lets it play with her jewellery;
beads running through its greedy fingers,
helping itself to scent.

She knows she'll never be rid of it,
has given up sex, summer tops, swimming,
taught it to massage away knots in her muscles,
made it earn its keep.

Weather
by Jennifer Copley

It broke the day after she died,
rain plummeting from purple clouds,
the force of the wind breaking their fence.
A black bin-bag blew up into the pear tree,
stayed snagged for eight years:

eight years since she went to bed early
saying surely tonight it would thunder,
her head was aching,
even the clock had clogged
in the sultry air.

He followed at his usual time,
found her restless, sheets bunched in her hands.
Are the windows closed? she said,
Is everything off? I'm worried about lightning.
Don't have a bath, it can spurt through the tap
and kill you.

Wardrobes
by Jennifer Copley

1 Free-standing, mahogany

Dark between his suits.
Dark in my memory.
A drawer marked Collars,
a drawer marked Studs.
One Army jacket with medals,
one Daks with elbow patches.
Striped ties roping me in
with the musty air.
A shelf for change – pennies,
halfpennies, threepenny bits.
Standing on his shoes,
standing in his shoes.
No one finding me,
no one squeezing in, saying Sardines.

2 Fitted, MDF

Could be the same inside
if you looked quickly –
familiar shirts and waistcoats,
sleeveless pullovers, a gabardine,
though corduroy trousers
have replaced the suits
and there's only one tie, kept knotted,
leaving just enough space for his head
and beaky nose.

You don't want to look up but you do –
on the top shelf, nappies,
a rubber sheet,
spare pyjamas (standard issue).

A portrait of V Nubiola
by Anne Berkeley

His red jacket buttons up a fury of muscle.
Everything's on the point of change,
only the soft popping of his lips as they draw on his pipe,
the engine of desire.
He leans his elbow on the table to stop it collapsing,
to maintain the balance between two apples.
He is furiously smoking to hold aloft
the miraculous circle, the memento mori
that hovers between pipe and decanter.
Even the tulip leans away, about to take flight.

I go into the room to straighten the table leg.
The heat is unbearable.
I ask him, what do you do when you're not sitting here
holding this impossible bubble in the air?
What debt do you owe, that you consent
to illustrate the Principle of Moments?
He cannot speak for the pipe;
if he grips any harder the stem will snap.
So long as he keeps smoking
his jacket will stay red, his rooftiles
will shrug off hailstones
and his hands will keep from necks and knives.

When I come out again bearing the decanter.
I unstopper it and smell – rough stuff
from down the southern end of the winelake.
The sort that doesn't travel.
I realise how much depends on him.

I leave behind the two apples:
one has a bad bruise on the side I can't see.
The other, on closer inspection,
isn't an apple at all.

Telling the weather
by Anne Berkeley

In the old coal cellar in the heart of the house
your workbench is piled with watch-glass and bottles,
tweezers and dials and lengths of straw.
Under the solitary bulb you burnish and fix
the job-lot of barometers, your apron stained
with wire-wool and fish-glue and sawdust.

You let me help, but sing sotto voce to tease me:
The sun has got his hat on
over and over, hamming it up till the damp
makes you wheeze, while I'm chasing
lost mercury in the dirt between tiles.
You sprinkle flowers of sulphur.

I draw the yard of glass upright in its case,
more gently than a clamp.
The tube trembles and twangs
as you unstopper the J,
settle pulley and weights
into a responsible column, to bear atmosphere.

You help me fix the awn to the back of the dial
which tells how damp it is outside
where rain might be blustering, for all I know.

Letter composed on a typewriter
by Rosie Blagg

She wouldn't let me see
what had been written –
what had made her cry.

The hammers had jabbed in so hard
a code of raised bumps
prickled through the thin blue paper.

Sometimes no-one spoke
when I answered the phone
but I knew the texture of secrets:

fusty as air inside an old piano –
acidic and heavy as the little bag of memory
digesting in my stomach.

Poem for a friend who skittered
by Rosie Blagg

She was clever and good
as a tall glass of cool water.
Her element was the sea
around the scraggled witch's boot
of Cornwall, Devon, Dorset.
A place of antiquated buildings,
college gardens could not hold her.

Childlike now, she counsels waitressing,
preventing the baby from drowning in the sink.
Two days ago, she sent me Mozart
through the post, with a poem.
She is expecting a child –
getting married soon.

A Shyness of Torches
by Rosie Blagg

Nocturnal by nature,
by day they are known
as a shyness of torches.

By night the torch seeks not
to illuminate, but to expose
the deeper darkness behind.

Companions
by Christy Ducker

His

Strapped in at birth,
you always need luggage
like these eleven plastic bags
you fill with toys
when told to pack for *School*.

Or this, the one blue tuck box,
pared down with steel trim.
If it slams, it will chop off
your little boy fingers.
Inside is your hoard of marbles,
baseball cards, and keys.
It sits beside a door that swings
on the breeze of a new country.

Hers

In one hand, a Moody's Meat bag
I go in for because it's blue,
because it will never snag a desk
like supermarket bags.
It will turn grey and die
when I want it to.
Inside are my schoolbooks,
backed in woodchip, a Braille purse
with two coins, a body spray saved
from last year. The teacher marks
my work and always comments on its smell.

In my other hand, a case that swings
from a chain handle, given to me
by a girl I don't know. She doesn't need it,
hears I'm *struggling*. The case holds
velvet, a flute in three pieces.
I can't keep the mouthpiece
in its slot. The lid is hard to close.

Anchorage
by Christy Ducker

His

It's the colour of the army
they tried to put you in,
this backpack of yours
that encompasses you.
It hulks against the cold
baring iodine, liquorice, petrol.
In the lid are tubing and filters,
a tent that rolls down
to the size of a small dog.
Stowed at its heart is a flint.

Alone out here, you'd live
on what you carry.

Hers

The zip on my pack's come loose,
but I still haven't lost the limes
I blagged from a bar in Tanunak.
They're under the tussling socks,
next to the bag of glass and honey
I'm saving for a dustbin.
My backpack is smaller than yours,
with lumps and bumps in Day-Glo
shades the wolves don't miss.
There's not a thing inside it
you'll ever ask to borrow.

Alone out here, I'd fall
on the kindness of strangers.

Do Not Disturb
by Christy Ducker

There were dead moths inside the clock at gran's,
whole drifts of them. She never knew because
the clock had stopped, its two hands kissing X.
No point in winding it, she'd say, *it is right
twice a day!* She liked the marble face of it,
would polish round like something going out
of fashion. The one time that I opened it,
I never let gran know. By night, I prised
the door, my fingers stumped among the works,
a dirty penny smell. I bumped a spring
and brought soft ticking into life, but caught
my thumb between two cogs that bit me, stopped
the clock.   Since then, I've let accumulate
the moths, the things that I could not quite right.

Cinnamon Press
Independent Innovative International

We hope you have enjoyed this book from Cinnamon Press.

Cinnamon publishes the **best in poetry, fiction and non-fiction**.

For writers – bi-annual competitions in four genres – first novel, novella, short story & first poetry collection. Cash prizes and publishing contracts.

For book lovers - great poetry and fiction titles from the best new names as well as established writers.

For the best amongst poetry journals: *Envoi* – celebrating 50 years of poetry

For a full list of titles visit: www.cinnamonpress.com

For the best amongst poetry journals:

Envoi

Now in large format, perfect bound full colour cover

Celebrating its 50th year of publication.

Envoi show-cases the best in poetry writing from writers in the UK and internationally, as well as carrying poetry features, competitions & essential poetry book reviews. The new *Envoi* website also features poetry & reviews.

For the best of both worlds:
Subscribe to *Envoi* and add an optional Cinnamon Poetry Book club subscription – three of our best new titles at discount prices, **available only to *Envoi* subscribers.**

www.envoipoetry.com